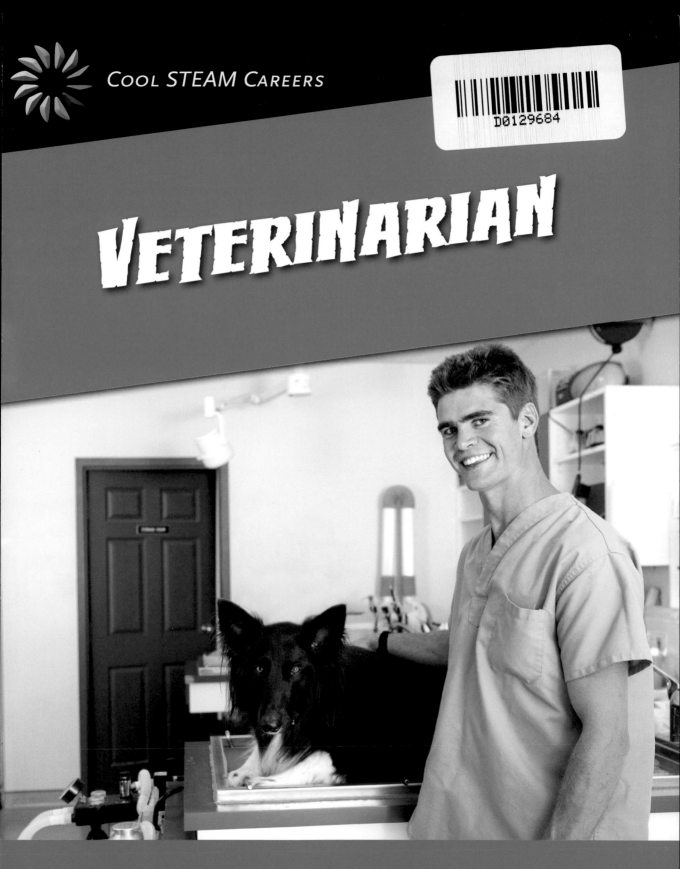

Cool STEAM Careers

Veterinarian

D0129684

BARBARA A. SOMERVILL

Published in the United States of America by Cherry Lake Publishing
Ann Arbor, Michigan
www.cherrylakepublishing.com

Content Adviser: Dr. Katherine Hughes, DVM
Reading Adviser: Marla Conn, ReadAbility, Inc.

Photo Credits: ©Tyler Olson/Shutterstock.com, cover, 1; ©elleon/iStock.com, 5; ©RGB Ventures/SuperStock/Alamy, 6; © Mimadeo/Shutterstock.com, 9; ©StockLike/Shutterstock Images, 10, 16; © Roger costa morera/Shutterstock.com, 13; © Vgstockstudio/Shutterstock.com, 15; © Shannon Fagan/Dreamstime.com, 17; ©annedde/iStock.com, 18; ©bikerider-london/Shutterstock.com, 21; ©pirita/Shutterstock.com, 22; ©Galina 2703/Shutterstock.com, 25; © Brandon Alms/Shutterstock.com, 26; ©Jen Grantham/Thinkstock, 29

Library of Congress Cataloging-in-Publication Data

Somervill, Barbara A., author.
  Veterinarian/Barbara A. Somervill.
    pages cm.—(Cool STEAM careers)
  Summary: "Readers will learn what it takes to succeed as a veterinarian. The book also explains the necessary educational steps, useful character traits, potential hazards, and daily job tasks related to this career. Sidebars include thought-provoking trivia. Questions in the backmatter ask for text-dependent analysis. Photos, a glossary, and additional resources are included."—Provided by publisher.
  Audience: Ages 8–12
  Audience: Grades 4 to 6
  Includes bibliographical references and index.
  ISBN 978-1-63362-566-2 (hardcover)—ISBN 978-1-63362-656-0 (pbk.)—ISBN 978-1-63362-746-8 (pdf)—ISBN 978-1-63362-836-6 (ebook)
  1. Veterinarians—Juvenile literature. 2. Veterinary medicine—Vocational guidance—Juvenile literature. I. Title.

SF756.S66 2016
636.089092—dc23
                          2014050353

Cherry Lake Publishing would like to acknowledge the work of the Partnership for 21st Century Skills. Please visit www.p21.org for more information.

Printed in the United States of America
Corporate Graphics

ABOUT THE AUTHOR

Barbara A. Somervill writes children's nonfiction books on a variety of topics. As a writer, she has had many different cool careers—teacher, news reporter, author, scriptwriter, and restaurant critic. She believes that researching new and different topics makes writing every book an adventure. When she is not writing, Ms. Somervill plays duplicate bridge, reads avidly, and travels.

TABLE OF CONTENTS

STEAM is the acronym for Science, Technology, Engineering, Arts, and Mathematics. In this book, you will read about how each of these study areas is connected to a career in veterinary medicine.

CHAPTER 1

How to Save a Life

A helicopter pilot sweeps across Kruger National Park in South Africa. Ahead, he spies a large bull elephant limping toward a stand of trees. The pilot radios to the park vet service, asking for a full vet ground team. He also asks for a second helicopter with a vet prepared to **tranquilize** the elephant.

The bull is traveling slowly, leading the group of older male elephants. The second helicopter arrives and hovers over them. The vet takes aim and fires a dart into the bull's flank. The tranquilizer takes effect quickly. Luckily, the elephant flops down on its left side with its injured leg exposed. The elephant's mates gather around to protect their herd leader, and the helicopter flies close to the ground to chase them away. Adult bull elephants can easily kill or injure humans,

Veterinarians work with all kinds of animals.

A vet can learn about an animal's health from listening to its heart, lungs, and gut.

so the vet team must make sure they are safe before tending to the bull's wounds.

The vet team discovers that poachers from a nearby village had shot the elephant with a poisoned arrow. While the elephant sleeps, the vet cleans the wound and removes dead tissue. After packing the wound with **antibiotics** and an **antidote** for the poison, the vet stitches the elephant's skin together. Although this is similar to when humans get stitches, the needle is much bigger and the stitching thread must be very strong. That's because the elephant's skin is thicker and tougher than human skin.

The elephant quickly recovers from the **anesthesia** and, although a bit shaky, rejoins his friends. This was the second elephant the vet team had saved from a poacher's poison that week. For a park vet, saving the lives of elephants is a normal part of the job.

THINK ABOUT ENGINEERING

The problem: Wild animals need to be controlled when injured. The solution: An injector dart is a highly technical device designed by engineers. The darts hold different amounts of anesthetic, depending on an animal's size. When the dart hits the animal, it automatically **injects** the medicine. This is one clever piece of engineering.

How Veterinary Medicine Began

Records of early **veterinary** efforts appear in an Egyptian medical textbook that is almost 4,000 years old. The book describes diseases of cattle, dogs, and birds. Other Egyptian texts describe animal **anatomy** and specific treatments. The Romans, Greeks, and Hebrews also had people who healed animals.

By the 1700s, people in Europe and North America wanted specialized doctors to take care of their animals. Farmers had to keep their livestock healthy. They depended on horses or mules for transportation. They sold cattle, sheep, or pigs to make money. They also wanted to prevent animals from spreading illness to humans. This led to the establishment of veterinary schools.

The first veterinary school was founded in Lyons, France, in 1761. Vets at the time worked mostly with

Throughout history vets have helped keep livestock healthy.

There are a growing number of women studying to be veterinarians.

farm animals, and their tools were very simple. Over the next decade, a few more schools were established throughout Europe. The first to open in the United States was one in Philadelphia in 1852, but it closed in 1866. Later, in 1883, the School of Veterinary Medicine at the University of Pennsylvania opened, and is still training students today.

Advances in veterinary medicine came with advances in human medicine. Eighty-five years ago, there were no antibiotics for humans or animals. Today, there are a wide range of antibiotics and medications specially made for animals to prevent heartworm, fleas, and ticks. Other medicines help lessen the pain that injured animals feel. Surgical instruments and techniques have improved, too. X-rays help vets **diagnose** such problems as broken bones, heart disease, or if an animal has eaten something it should not have eaten. An **ultrasound** shows problems with internal organs, bones, and muscles. A modern vet's office has much of the same equipment as a modern doctor's office.

THINK ABOUT ART

A growing field of art is veterinary medical illustration. Detailed veterinary illustrations are important for vet students to learn about the muscle structure, veins, arteries, bones, and nerves of various species of animals. There are more than 2,000 medical illustrators in the United States, but very few deal with veterinary illustration. If art and animals fascinate you, perhaps you might consider this new art field.

In 1930, only 30 women in the United States were veterinarians. Fifty years ago, veterinary medicine was described as "no job for a lady." Most people felt that handling animals, especially large farm animals, required a man's strength. According to the American Veterinary Medical Association, women now account for more than half of the association's 75,000 vets. Today, both male and female vets are helping provide quality health care to animals everywhere.

As with doctors, vets often specialize in specific areas of animal care. There are large animal vets, small animal vets, exotic animal vets, veterinary surgeons, and emergency care specialists. Sometimes vets specialize in heart care, eye care, and the skin care of animals. There are also vet dentists. Veterinary medicine for birds and reptiles is growing, and some scientists develop medicine to heal parrots, iguanas, or grizzly bears.

Vets receive specialized training to care for a wide variety of animals.

CHAPTER 3

A VET'S JOB

The phone rings at 1:30 a.m. A vet is called to assist a mare having trouble **foaling**. Being called in the middle of the night is not too unusual. The vet arrives at the horse stables at 2:30 a.m. It is dark and cold, and the vet is tired, but those things do not matter. What's important is the health of the mare and her baby. The delivery takes a little more than three hours. It's a girl!

After the delivery, there is time for a quick shower and breakfast before heading to the office. This morning, the vet has a full appointment book. The first

Giving a vaccine shot to a cat is just part of a vet's daily work.

three patients need surgery. A dog is being spayed—
an operation that prevents female animals from
having babies. A male cat needs a tumor removed.
Finally, a playful dog needs anesthesia to have a broken
tooth pulled.

Later, a beagle puppy comes in for its shots. Vets give
animals **vaccines** to prevent diseases. Puppies and
kittens usually get these when they're just a few months
old. These shots are like the ones that human children
get from their doctors. As the day wears on, the vet

Some vets may look at pet rabbits.

examines and treats dogs and cats of all ages. The vet even sees a parrot with a broken wing.

After lunch, a large dog comes in with a serious laceration, or tear, in its skin. The wound must be examined carefully and cleaned. To make sure that the dog feels no pain, the vet gives it a shot of anesthetic. The wound is stitched and bandaged, and the dog is sent home with antibiotics to prevent infection. With time to heal, the dog will be just fine.

During free time, the vet visits the surgery patients from earlier in the day. The vet takes their temperatures and listens to their breathing. Blood test results for three of yesterday's patients have arrived from the lab. The vet reviews the reports and calls the pet owners to pick up needed medicine.

Sometimes animals who are recovering from surgery may have to stay at the vet's office overnight.

Advances in technology allow vets to provide even better care to animals.

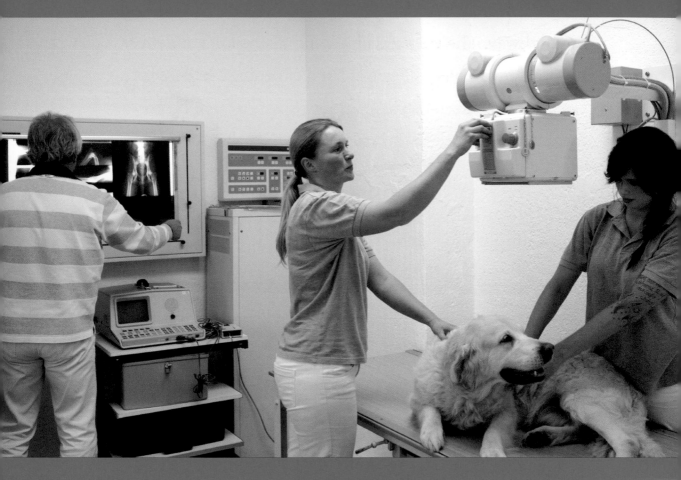

[21ST CENTURY SKILLS LIBRARY]

Late in the day, a call comes in from the local humane society. A dog wounded by a car was found on the highway. The vet team clears out a surgical room. X-rays show the dog's leg is broken. The dog's leg is set, and the vet's day comes to an end. It is 6:30 p.m. The vet does a quick check of the animals that will be cared for overnight. It has been a long day but very rewarding. The vet has used experience and training to help many animals.

THINK ABOUT TECHNOLOGY

Veterinarians use technology that is similar to what doctors use on humans. Vets diagnose problems using x-ray machines, ultrasound machines, and laboratory testing equipment. Laser therapy is used to treat tissue injuries and to promote wound healing.

CHAPTER 4

THE ROAD TO A CAREER

Becoming a vet can be more challenging than becoming a doctor or dentist, because there are so few vet schools, and therefore fewer openings for students to apply to. Only the top students are accepted, and those students come from all over the world. Potential vets must first earn an undergraduate degree for which they study mathematics, chemistry, biology, and physical science. Students who apply to vet school take the Veterinary Aptitude Test (VAT), Medical College Admission Test (MCAT), or the Graduate Record

A recommendation from a professor may be necessary to be accepted into vet school.

Examination (GRE). These tests are usually given to college students before they graduate. Acceptance into vet school depends on a student's grades, activities, recommendations from professors, and the results on these tests.

The American Veterinary Medical Association certifies 30 colleges and schools of veterinary medicine in the United States and 5 in Canada. These schools meet the standards for quality veterinary learning. In the first two years, students learn about topics such as

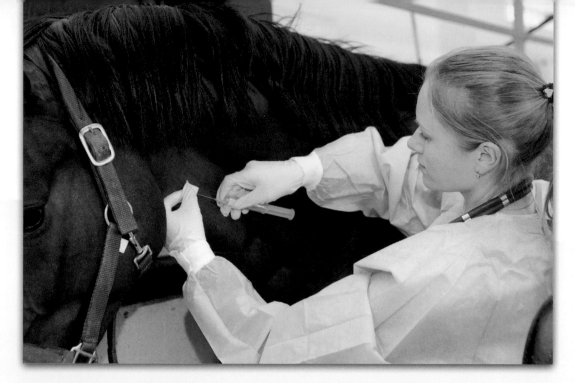

One skill vet students practice is drawing blood.

animal anatomy, medicines, and veterinary **ethics**. They begin learning how to use technology for diagnosing diseases and are trained in specific techniques for certain procedures and surgeries performed on animals.

A student's last two years include more hands-on experience in a clinic with animals. Students treat animals and perform surgery under the supervision of licensed veterinarians, instructors, and technicians. This helps students gain valuable experience. By graduation, each student will have spent about 4,000 hours in the classroom and laboratory and doing clinical studies. Each year, slightly more than 2,000 new vets receive Doctor of Veterinary Medicine (DVM, or, at the University of Pennsylvania, VMD) degrees in the United States. Each vet must be licensed in the state where he or she practices.

Setting up a vet's practice is expensive. Vets need rooms for examining and treating animals. They need operating rooms and the instruments for surgery, as well as x-ray equipment. They also need to stock veterinary medicines. It is all worthwhile when an animal is saved.

THINK ABOUT MATH

If you wonder when you might use algebra in real life, become a vet and you will find out. Mathematics is an important aspect of veterinary medicine. The amount of medication, food, or anesthesia an animal needs depends on both the species of animal and the animal's weight. It is important to make accurate calculations when caring for every animal.

CHAPTER 5

A FUTURE WITH ANIMALS

Today, most vets treat small household pets, such as cats and dogs. This is called a small-animal practice. Other vets specialize in farm animals, such as horses, cattle, goats, and sheep. Yet other vets treat exotic animals, such as large birds, reptiles, apes, and tigers. They work in zoos, aquariums, and nature preserves.

An exotic animal vet must know how to treat many species of animals. Some animals, such as pandas, are in danger of becoming extinct. Exotic animal vets help them reproduce and stay healthy. They also care for animals in circuses, safari parks, national parks, and zoos.

Marine vets are also involved in exotic medicine. Marine vets usually work in aquariums, but they can work for **aquaculture** farms or marine conservation groups as well.

About 2,000 vets work for the federal government in the Departments of Agriculture, Defense, and Health

A zoo vet may have different responsibilities than a vet who works in a clinic.

An aquarium may have a vet on staff to examine animals, treat injuries, and perform surgeries.

[21ST CENTURY SKILLS LIBRARY]

Services. They inspect meat and poultry and help prevent the spread of disease by animals. Vets may do research on animal and human diseases. They test the safety of various medications or chemicals used on animals, on people, and in the environment. They may work with pet food companies or care for animals used in medical research. Researchers might also work to discover better ways to treat certain conditions.

Many vets participate in animal rescue projects. These projects are designed to save wild animals that are found wounded or sick. These projects may also

THINK ABOUT SCIENCE

Veterinary medicine involves several different sciences: anatomy, nutrition, medicine, and zoology. If a career as a vet is in your future, begin by studying biology, zoology, genetics, and anatomy in school. These sciences form the foundation of veterinary medicine.

rescue pets that are abandoned, injured, or lost in disasters. Animals—both in homes and in the wild—need human help. Helping animals begins by taking good care of your own pets. Just as people need doctors and regular medical checkups, so do household pets. Vets provide health care advice, recommend medicines, and suggest ways to better care for animals.

Volunteers can work with vets in animal rescue programs. Volunteers help in nature preserves and animal shelters. These experiences give an inside look at a career in veterinary medicine. Anyone interested in becoming a vet needs to work hard and have a love and appreciation for animals. Volunteering is one way to find out if a career helping animals suits you.

Volunteering at a zoo, farm, or vet clinic is a good way to see if a career as a veterinarian might be a good fit for you.

THINK ABOUT IT

According to the American Veterinary Medicine Association, vets in the United States care for 70 million dogs, 80 million cats, 11 million birds, 5 million horses, and a variety of other animals. Which pets do you think are the easiest to treat? Which ones do you think are the hardest? Defend your answer.

What is the connection between human medicine and veterinary medicine? Make a list of ways these two fields are similar. Reread chapters 2 and 3 for some ideas.

Do you have a pet? Go with your parents to the next vet appointment. If you don't have a pet, see if you can go with the family of a friend who has a pet. Talk to the vet. What does he or she like most about the job? Which parts of the job are the hardest?

LEARN MORE

FURTHER READING

Jackson, Donna M. *ER Vets: Life in an Animal Emergency Room.* Boston: HMH Books for Young Readers, 2009.

Riddle, John, and Rae Simmons. *Veterinarian.* Broomall, PA: Mason Crest, 2014.

Trout, Nick. *Tell Me Where It Hurts: A Day of Humor, Healing, and Hope in My Life as an Animal Surgeon.* New York: Broadway Books, 2009.

Wells, Jeff. *All My Patients Have Tales: Favorite Stories from a Vet's Practice.* New York: St. Martin's Griffin, 2010.

WEB SITES

Bureau of Labor Statistics
www.bls.gov/ooh/healthcare/veterinarians.htm
Find out about the jobs vets do, how much they are paid, and what the outlook is for vet jobs.

Love That Pet
https://www.lovethatpet.com/
Explore this website for advice about taking care of your cat, dog, or other pet.

Veterinarians Without Borders
www.vetswithoutbordersus.org
Learn how vets help care for animals throughout the world.

GLOSSARY

anatomy (uh-NAT-uh-mee) study of the physical structure of a body, including muscles, bones, and organs

anesthesia (an-iss-THEE-szuh) medicine that makes a patient insensitive to pain

antibiotics (an-ti-bye-OT-iks) medicine that kills infection caused by bacteria

antidote (AN-ti-doht) the cure for a poison

aquaculture (AK-wuh-kuhl-cher) the cultivation of aquatic organisms (especially fish or shellfish), especially for food

diagnose (dye-uhg-NOHS) to identify an illness or medical condition

ethics (ETH-iks) a code of good conduct

foaling (FOL-ing) giving birth to a foal

injects (in-JEKTS) puts medicine into a person's or animal's body through a needle

tranquilize (TRANG-kwuhl-ize) to give a medicine that calms a patient

ultrasound (UHL-truh-sound) sound whose frequency is too high for the human ear to hear; ultrasound waves are sounds used to create images in medical scans

vaccines (vak-SEENZ) medicines that prevent animals and people from contracting diseases

veterinary (VET-ur-uh-ner-ee) dealing with the diseases or medical conditions of animals

INDEX